Cyber Savvy: A Parent's Guide to Protecting Kids' Online Privacy

As parents, it is our responsibility to not only raise our children to be kind, responsible, and successful individuals, but also to protect them from the dangers that exist in the world around us. Today, one of the most significant threats to our children's well-being is the internet and technology.

The internet is a powerful tool that can provide our children with a wealth of knowledge and opportunities, but it also exposes them to a host of risks, including cyberbullying, sexting, and online predators. As parents, it is our job to educate ourselves about these risks and to teach our children how to use technology safely and responsibly.

This is where "Raising Safe Surfers: A Guide to Protecting Kids Online" comes in. This book provides parents with the knowledge and tools they need to keep their children safe online. It covers a wide range of topics, including setting up parental controls, monitoring your child's online activity, and having open and honest conversations with your children about internet safety.

As you read this book, you will gain a better understanding of the dangers that exist online and learn how to take proactive steps to protect your children. You will also learn about the many resources available to parents to help them navigate the digital world with confidence.

We live in a digital age where technology is an integral part of our lives. As parents, it is our responsibility to ensure that our children are safe as they navigate this ever-changing landscape. "Raising Safe Surfers: A Guide to Protecting Kids Online" is an essential tool to help us do just that. It will empower you to be informed and proactive in keeping your children safe online. We strongly recommend it as a resource to all parents, guardians and educators.

ChatGPT's guidance was a literary muse for this booklet's creation.

content

Chapter 1. Introduction to online privacy and safety

Online privacy refers to the ability of an individual or organization to keep their personal or business information private while using the internet. It is important to protect your online privacy because, without it, you may be vulnerable to cyber attacks, identity theft, and other forms of online abuse.

There are several ways to protect your online privacy, including:

1. Using strong and unique passwords:
It is important to use strong passwords that are difficult for hackers to guess or crack. A strong password should be at least 8 characters long and include a combination of upper and lower case letters, numbers, and special characters. It is also important to use unique passwords for each of your online accounts. This way, if one password is compromised, the attacker will not be able to access your other accounts using the same password. A password manager can help you generate and store strong, unique passwords for all of your accounts.

2. Securing your device:
Keeping your device up to date with the latest security patches and antivirus software is essential for protecting against cyber threats. Security patches are updates that fix vulnerabilities in your operating system or software, while antivirus software helps to protect against malware such as viruses, worms, and Trojan horses. Make sure to regularly update your device and install reputable antivirus software to ensure the best protection.

3. Being cautious when sharing personal information:
When sharing personal information online, it is important to be selective about what you reveal. Think about whether the information you are sharing is necessary and consider the potential risks of sharing it. For example, sharing your full name, birthdate, and home address on a social media profile could make it easier for an attacker to steal your identity. It is also a good idea to check the privacy settings on your social media accounts and adjust them to the highest level of protection.

4. Using a VPN:
A virtual private network (VPN) is a tool that encrypts your internet connection and hides your IP address. This can help protect your online activity from being monitored by hackers or third parties, and can be especially useful when using public Wi-Fi networks. When you connect to a VPN, all of your internet traffic is routed through a secure server, making it more difficult for anyone to intercept or track your online activity.

Online safety refers to the measures you take to protect yourself and your devices from online threats, such as cyber attacks and malicious software. Some tips for staying safe online include:

1. Keeping your device and software up to date:
As mentioned above, it is important to keep your device and software up to date with the latest security patches and antivirus software to protect against cyber threats.

2. Being cautious when clicking on links:
Be careful when clicking on links, especially if you receive them through email or social media. They could be malicious and lead you to a website that could harm your device or steal your personal information.

3. Avoiding suspicious websites:
Be cautious when visiting websites, especially ones that you are not familiar with. They could contain malware or phishing scams that can harm your device or steal your personal information.

4. Protecting your devices when using public Wi-Fi:
Public Wi-Fi networks can be vulnerable to cyber attacks, so it is important to use a VPN when using them to protect your device and personal information.

By following these tips and taking steps to protect your online privacy and safety, you can help reduce the risk of falling victim to cyber threats and other forms of online abuse.

Chapter 2. Understanding personal information and how it can be used online

Personal information is any information that can be used to identify an individual. This can include things like your name, address, phone number, email address, and date of birth. Personal information is often collected and stored by companies and organizations in order to provide services, communicate with customers, or for other business purposes.

When you use the internet, you may be asked to provide personal information in order to create an account, make a purchase, or access certain services. It is important to be mindful of the personal information you share online and to only provide what is necessary.

There are a few key ways that personal information can be used online:

1. Marketing and advertising:
Companies may use your personal information to tailor advertisements and marketing materials to your interests. For example, if you have searched for a particular product online, you may start seeing ads for that product on other websites you visit.

2. Personalization:
Many websites and apps use personal information to provide a personalized experience. For example, a music streaming service may use your listening history to recommend new artists or songs.

3. Fraud prevention:
Personal information can be used to verify your identity and prevent fraud. For example, if you make a purchase online, the company may ask for your name and billing address to confirm that you are the rightful owner of the credit card being used.

4. Data analytics:
Personal information can also be used for data analytics, which involves analyzing large sets of data to uncover trends and patterns. This can be used for a variety of purposes, such as improving products and services or identifying potential problems.

It is important to be aware of how your personal information may be used online and to carefully read the privacy policies of websites and apps before providing your personal information. You can also adjust your privacy settings on social media platforms and other online services to control the personal information that is shared.

By understanding how your personal information can be used online and taking steps to protect it, you can help ensure that your personal information is not misused or exposed to potential risks.

Chapter 3.   Creating and using strong passwords

In today's digital age, it's more important than ever to protect your online accounts with strong, unique passwords. A strong password is one that is difficult for others to guess or crack. It should be a combination of letters, numbers, and special characters, and should be at least 8 characters long.

When it comes to creating and using strong passwords, there are several best practices that can help ensure the security of online accounts. Here are a few key points that you might consider:

1.   Use a mix of upper and lowercase letters, numbers, and special characters in your passwords. The more complex a password is, the more difficult it will be for someone to guess or crack.

2.   Avoid using easily guessable information, such as your name, address, or common words, in your passwords. Instead, try using a phrase or a series of random words that are easy for you to remember but difficult for others to guess.

3.   Avoid using the same password across multiple accounts. If one of your accounts is compromised, using the same password on other accounts means that all of them are at risk.

4.   Encourage children to use passphrases instead of password, which are more easier to remember and hard to crack.

5.   Consider using a password manager to securely store and generate unique, complex passwords for different accounts.

6.   Educate children about the importance of protecting their passwords and keeping them secret, and teach them to be skeptical of anyone asking for their password, even if the person appears to be someone they know or trust.

7.   Encourage children to enable two-factor authentication wherever possible as an added layer of security to their accounts.

8.   It's also important to note that with the evolution of technology, the way of cracking the passwords has also evolved like using AI and Machine Learning, so it's important to keep updating the information and best practices to stay ahead.

9.   One way to create a strong password is to use a passphrase. A passphrase is a sequence of words or other text that can be easily remembered but is difficult for others to guess. For example, instead of using the password "password123," a passphrase like "mydog#1isFluffy" is much stronger.

10.   Another method for creating a strong password is to use a combination of random characters, numbers, and symbols. This can be difficult to remember, so it's important to write it down and store it in a secure location. It's also a good idea to use a password manager, it allows you to store all your passwords in an encrypted database, that can be accessed with one master password, so you don't have to remember all different passwords you use.

11.   It's also important to remember not to share your passwords with anyone. You should change your passwords regularly, especially for accounts related to financial or sensitive information.

One common tactic used by cybercriminals to gain access to your online accounts is Phishing Scams. It is important to be wary of clicking on any links or entering any personal information on a website unless you trust and know it's legitimate.

In summary, using weak or easily guessable passwords can leave you vulnerable to cyber attacks, identity theft, and other malicious activities. It's important to use strong, unique passwords for all of your online accounts and take the necessary steps to protect your personal information. Teach your kids to do the same, so they can stay safe online.

Chapter 4.   Protecting against online scams and fraud

In this Chapter we discuss the various ways in which scammers and fraudsters operate online and how to protect children from falling victim to their schemes.

One common tactic used by scammers is phishing, which involves sending fake emails or messages that appear to be from legitimate organizations or individuals, such as banks or government agencies. These messages often ask for personal information, such as login credentials or social security numbers, and may contain links to fake websites that look like the real thing. To protect children from phishing scams, it's important to teach them to never click on links or enter personal information into a website unless they are certain it is legitimate.

Another tactic used by scammers is social engineering, which involves using psychological tricks to manipulate people into giving away personal information or money. For example, a scammer may impersonate a grandchild in distress and ask for money to be wired to them. To protect children from social engineering scams, it's important to teach them to be skeptical of unsolicited requests for personal information or money, and to verify the identity of anyone who makes such a request.

Another way of scammers to operate is through Online fraud such as, through sale of fake or counterfeit items, or using fake online store or website. To protect children from these type of scams, is important to teach them to always be cautious when making online purchases, and to stick to well-known and reputable online retailers and marketplaces.

It is also important to teach children to recognize and report suspicious activity online, such as messages from strangers that make them feel uncomfortable or websites that ask for personal information without a good reason. By educating children about the various types of online scams and fraud, and equipping them with the knowledge and skills to protect themselves, you can help keep them safe as they navigate the digital world.

Additionally, Parents should also be aware of the software and application that their children uses, to filter and restrict access to certain website and monitor their online activities.

It's also important to practice security habits at home such as keeping software updated, creating strong passwords and not sharing them with anyone, and being cautious when giving out personal information online.

Lastly, It's important to remember that scammers are constantly developing new tactics to defraud people, so it's important to stay informed and to continue to educate children about online safety on a regular basis.

Chapter 5.   Safely using social media and messaging apps

It is important to discuss the ways in which social media and messaging apps can be used safely. Social media and messaging apps can be a great way for kids to stay connected with friends and family, but they can also present risks if not used properly. Here are some key points to consider when discussing the safe use of social media and messaging apps with children:

1. Privacy settings: Make sure that kids understand the importance of adjusting privacy settings on their social media accounts. They should know that they can control who can see their posts, messages, and personal information.

2. Be mindful of what you post: Encourage kids to be mindful of the content they post on social media. Remind them that once something is posted online, it can be difficult to remove and can have long-lasting consequences.

3.   Be aware of "phishing" scam: They should be cautious about clicking on links from unknown sources, which could be a phishing scam, These scammers use emails, text messages and social media post, to trick people into providing personal information, passwords or money.

4.   Cyberbullying: Talk to kids about the importance of treating others online with kindness and respect. They should know that cyberbullying is not acceptable and how to report if they see it happening or experience it themselves

5.   Stranger danger: Remind kids that not everyone they interact with online is who they say they are. Teach them to never meet in person with someone they met online without your permission and supervision.

6.   Time management: Set guidelines for how much time kids are allowed to spend on social media and messaging apps. Encourage them to balance their online activities with other interests and responsibilities.

It is essential for parents to stay involved in their child's online activities and to have open and honest conversations with them about the potential risks associated with social media and messaging apps. By following these guidelines, parents can help their children navigate the digital world safely.

It would also be a good idea to consider including a section about parental controls, like setting up boundaries for apps and monitoring the activity on the device. Also, encourage your kids to think twice before sharing personal information online, such as contact numbers and location.

Chapter 6. Cyberbullying prevention and response

Cyberbullying is a serious problem that affects many children and teenagers who use the internet and social media. It can take many forms, including sending threatening or hurtful messages, spreading rumors, and sharing embarrassing photos or videos.

Preventing cyberbullying begins with educating children and teenagers about the dangers of cyberbullying and how to protect themselves. Parents and teachers should talk to children and teenagers about the importance of being kind and respectful online, and should encourage them to speak up if they or someone they know is being bullied.

There are several strategies that can be used to prevent cyberbullying. One strategy is to teach children and teenagers about the importance of privacy and security online. This can include setting privacy settings on social media accounts and using strong passwords.

Another strategy is to teach children and teenagers about the consequences of cyberbullying. This can include discussing legal consequences, such as charges of harassment or cyberstalking, as well as the social and emotional consequences for the victim and the bully.

Another aspect of prevention is that parents and teachers should also monitor the child's online activity and know the who, what and when of the child activity.

Additionally, parents and teachers can help to create a positive and supportive online community. This can include encouraging children and teenagers to be positive role models online, and promoting healthy and respectful communication.

When it comes to response, it is important to have a clear plan in place for addressing cyberbullying incidents. This can include identifying a trusted adult or resource that children and teenagers can turn to if they are bullied. This can be a school counselor or a parent, for example.

Another important part of response is to document the evidence of the bullying, such as screenshots of hurtful messages or posts. This can be used to present the case to the school or legal authorities.

It is also important to work with the victim to provide support and resources. This can include counseling and social-emotional support, and connecting the victim with resources such as a helpline or online support group.

It is also important to take action against the bully, which can include disciplinary action by the school or legal consequences. However, it's essential to consider the bully's perspective and help him or her understand the impacts of their actions, also they might need support and guidance on how to change their behavior.

In summary, preventing and responding to cyberbullying requires a multifaceted approach that includes educating children and teenagers about the dangers of cyberbullying, promoting positive and supportive online communities, and having a clear plan in place for addressing incidents of cyberbullying.

Chapter 7.   Keeping devices and software up to date

Keeping devices and software up to date is an important aspect of maintaining the security and privacy of you and your family's online activities. Here are some key points you might want to consider:

1.   Software updates often include important security patches that address known vulnerabilities in the software. Installing these updates in a timely manner can help protect against potential attacks and data breaches.

2.   Many devices, such as smartphones and tablets, have automatic updates turned on by default. However, it's still a good idea to check for updates regularly and install them as soon as they become available.

3.   Some devices and software, particularly older models or products that are no longer supported by the manufacturer, may not receive updates at all. In this case, it's important to consider replacing these devices or software with more up-to-date and secure options.

4.   Some software, such as antivirus and anti-malware programs, are particularly important to keep updated. These types of programs rely on regular updates to their malware definitions in order to effectively detect and remove known threats.

5.   Keeping devices and software up to date can also improve their performance and add new features. So in addition to security benefits, updating can also enhance the user experience.

6.   Be aware of phishing attempts or scam emails, which can be sent from hackers and cybercriminals. They may ask you to click a link to update your software or device and will redirect you to a malicious website, where your personal information can be compromised. So always be sure to update from official sources and check the link before you click.

7.   Educating family members, particularly children, about the importance of keeping devices and software up to date, and providing them with clear instructions on how to check for and install updates can help them stay safer online.

8.   With the increasing number of IoT devices, the need to update the devices and software have been increased, educate family members on the importance of keeping all connected device such as smart TVs, cameras, routers, speakers and others updated to avoid any security risks.

In summary, Keeping devices and software up to date is a critical step in protecting against online threats and maintaining the security and privacy of your family's online activities.

Chapter 8.   Using the internet responsibly and ethically

The focus is on teaching children how to use the internet responsibly and ethically.

The internet has become an integral part of modern life, and it's important for children to learn how to use it responsibly and ethically. This chapter will cover some key concepts related to responsible and ethical internet use, including:

1. Digital citizenship: Digital citizenship refers to the responsible and ethical use of technology. It includes understanding the importance of online safety, privacy, and security, as well as the importance of being respectful and considerate in online interactions.

2. Netiquette: Netiquette refers to the rules of etiquette that apply to online communication. It includes things like not sharing personal information with strangers, not bullying or being mean to others online, and not plagiarizing or stealing others' work.

3. Privacy: Privacy is an important issue online, as personal information can be easily shared and spread. It's important for children to understand the importance of keeping their personal information private and not sharing it with strangers or posting it online.

4. Cyberbullying: Cyberbullying is the use of technology to harass, threaten, or bully others. It's important for children to understand the negative effects of cyberbullying and the importance of not engaging in such behavior.

5. Plagiarism: Plagiarism is the act of using someone else's work without giving credit. It's important for children to understand the importance of proper citation and not plagiarizing when using information found online.

6. Online Safety: It is important for children to understand the risks of online activities such as downloading unknown files or clicking on unsolicited links.

One important aspect of responsible internet use is being aware of and actively working to prevent cyberbullying. This can include not participating in or encouraging harmful behavior online, as well as speaking up and reporting any instances of cyberbullying that one may witness. It's also important to teach children how to handle cyberbullying if it happens to them, whether that be through blocking the perpetrator, reaching out to a trusted adult, or using other coping mechanisms.

Another important aspect of responsible internet use is protecting one's online privacy. This includes being mindful of the personal information that is shared online, using strong passwords, and being cautious of phishing scams and other malicious activities. Additionally, it's crucial to be aware of and comply with the terms of service and privacy policies of the websites and apps that are being used.

In addition to these practical considerations, it's also important to teach children about digital the responsible and ethical use of technology. This includes being respectful of others online, understanding and adhering to copyright laws, and knowing how to responsibly engage with online content, including the ability to distinguish between credible sources and misinformation.

It's also important to note the responsibility to respect others online and not to engage in any discriminatory or harmful content or speech. Especially with the rise of social media, it's important to be aware of the impact that one's words and actions can have on others and to strive to be a positive and respectful member of the online community.

This chapter, parents and educators will find recommendations, resources and tips to help children use the internet responsibly and ethically. The goal is to empower kids to make safe and responsible choices online and to develop critical thinking skills that will serve them well in the digital age.

Overall, it is important to teach kids to use the internet in a responsible and ethical manner, which include all the above concepts. The parent/guardian/teacher should lead by example, modeling appropriate online behavior and discussing these topics with their children regularly. This guide should be used as a tool to start conversations and to help children develop the skills they need to use the internet responsibly and ethically.

It is important to have open communication, to let them know you are there to help them in difficult situations and to establish proper use of internet policies in your home.

Chapter 9. Safely using public Wi-Fi networks

This is an important topic in the context of protecting children online. Public Wi-Fi networks can be found in many places such as airports, coffee shops, hotels, and libraries, and they can be very convenient for kids and families who need to use the internet while on the go. However, these networks can also pose significant security risks, as they are often unsecured and easily accessible to hackers.

One of the main risks of using public Wi-Fi networks is that they may not be encrypted, which means that any data sent or received over the network can be intercepted and read by anyone on the same network. This includes personal information such as login credentials, passwords, and credit card numbers, as well as sensitive information like private messages and emails.

To protect kids from these risks, it's important to teach them to use a virtual private network (VPN) when connecting to public Wi-Fi networks. A VPN encrypts all data sent and received over the network, making it much more difficult for hackers to intercept and read. Additionally, it will mask the IP address and location of the user, making it harder to trace or track.

Another important step is to make sure that the device used to connect to the public Wi-Fi network has up-to-date anti-virus and anti-malware software installed. This will help protect against any malicious software that may be present on the network.

It is also important to educate kids on being cautious about clicking on links and opening attachments from unknown sources, as well as not sharing too much personal information over the network. Public Wi-Fi networks can be convenient, but it's important to be aware of the risks and take the necessary precautions to protect against them.

In addition, to ensure their complete safety on public Wi-Fi, parents can also use a monitoring software to keep an eye on the activities of their children over the internet, on any device. This will help in keeping the internet activities of their kids under check and also keep a tab on the websites and apps that their children visit.

In short, the key takeaways for this chapter includes educating kids about the risks of public Wi-Fi networks, teaching them how to use a VPN, to keep the device and anti-virus software up-to-date, to be cautious about clicking on links and attachments from unknown sources, not sharing personal information over the network and use of parental monitoring software.

Chapter 10.   Protecting against online predators and strangers

HARIK HACK

Online safety is a critical issue, especially when it comes to protecting children from predators and strangers. In this chapter, we will discuss the steps parents and caregivers can take to ensure that kids are safe while they are online.

First and foremost, education is key. It is important to teach children about the dangers of the internet, including the risks associated with sharing personal information, the importance of privacy, and the fact that not everyone on the internet is who they say they are. Explain to them that there are people who may try to trick or harm them, and that it's important to be cautious and aware of their surroundings online.

Open and honest communication is also essential. Encourage your child to talk to you about their online activities, including the websites they visit, the people they talk to, and the things they do online. Let them know that they can come to you if they feel uncomfortable or if something happens that they don't understand This will help build trust between you and your child and make them more likely to come to you if they encounter any problems online.

Monitoring is another important aspect of online safety. Consider using monitoring software to keep track of your child's online activities. These programs can help you see what websites they visit, who they talk to, and what they do online. It's also important to have a conversation with your child about monitoring and explain to them why you are using it, this will help them understand your concerns and avoid any mistrust.

It is also important to make sure that your child knows how to adjust their privacy settings on the websites and apps they use. Explain to them that privacy settings can help protect their personal information and limit who can see their online activity.

In addition, educate your child on the importance of being selective when it comes to friending and contacting people online. Tell them not to accept friend requests or messages from people they don't know, and to be cautious about sharing personal information with people they do know but have not met in person.

If your child encounters any suspicious or concerning behavior online, it is important to encourage them to report it. Show them how to use the "report" or "flag" feature on websites and apps, and explain to them that it's important to tell a trusted adult if they see something that makes them uncomfortable.

Lastly, set-up rules and agreement with your child is an important step. Have a talk with them and set-up specific rules and boundaries that they need to follow. Make sure they understand and agreed with the rules. This can be a good starting point for discussing the dangers of the internet and for your child to understand that you are taking their online safety seriously.

It is important to remember that as technology and the internet continue to evolve, so do the ways in which predators and strangers may try to harm children online. Staying informed and vigilant is key to keeping children safe. By following the guidelines outlined in this chapter, parents and caregivers can help ensure that their children have a safe and enjoyable experience while they are online.

Chapter 11.   Managing online friendships and relationships

In today's digital age, children are spending more and more time online, connecting with friends and strangers alike. While the internet can be a great tool for socializing and learning, it also poses risks to children's safety and well-being. Managing online friendships and relationships is an important aspect of keeping children safe while they are online. In this chapter, we will discuss some key points that parents and caregivers should keep in mind when it comes to children's online interactions.

1.   Emphasizing the difference between online and offline friendships: One of the first things parents and caregivers should do is educate children on the difference between online and offline friendships. Online friendships are those that are formed through the internet and are often maintained through electronic communication such as instant messaging, social media, and email. Offline friendships, on the other hand, are those that are formed in person and are maintained through face-to-face interaction. It's essential to educate children on how to navigate both types of friendships safely. Encourage them to think critically about the people they interact with online, and to be aware that online relationships may not be as genuine as those in the real world.

2.   Discussing the potential of catfishing: Another important aspect of managing online friendships and relationships is discussing the potential of catfishing. Catfishing is when someone creates a fake identity online to trick someone into a relationship. This is a common practice used by predators to target children. Parents and caregivers should educate children about the potential of catfishing and how to avoid it. Explain to them to be careful of people who they've never met in person and to be skeptical of overly friendly strangers online.

3.   Setting boundaries: Just like in the real world, it's important to set boundaries when it comes to online relationships. Encourage children to be cautious when sharing personal information, and to be mindful of the information they share about themselves and others online. This includes not sharing sensitive information such as their home address or phone number, and not posting pictures or videos that could put them at risk.

4.   Discussing the effects of social media on self-esteem: Social media can have a big impact on children's self-esteem, both positively and negatively. It is important for parents to discuss how social media usage can affect how children feel about themselves and how it can also affect their online relationships. Encourage children to be mindful of the content they post and the people they interact with online, and to take breaks from social media if they start to feel overwhelmed or negative.

5.   Encouraging healthy online communication: Encourage children to communicate with their online friends in a positive and respectful manner, and to avoid engaging in cyberbullying or other negative behavior. This includes not spreading rumors or gossip online, not posting negative or hurtful comments, and not engaging in online harassment or bullying.

6.   Encouraging to meet their online friends in person: Encourage children to meet their online friends in person, especially if the relationship has been going on for some time, and the opportunity arises. This can help to build stronger connections and also will reduce the risks of online predation.

7.   Reminding of the importance of privacy: Remind children to be aware of their privacy settings and to not share personal information with anyone they do not know or trust. This includes not accepting friend requests from strangers and not sharing personal information such as their home address or phone number.

8. Discussing the potential of addiction: Discuss with your children the potential risks of addiction with social media and how to manage their usage and time spent on it. Encourage them to set limits on their social media use and to take regular breaks from their screens. Remind them that it's important to balance their time spent online with other activities, such as exercise, reading, and spending time with family and friends.

Managing online friendships and relationships can be challenging, especially for children who are still learning about the complexities of social interactions. By educating them about the dangers of the internet, setting clear boundaries, and fostering healthy online communication, parents and caregivers can help keep children safe while they navigate the online world.

In conclusion, managing online friendships and relationships is an important aspect of keeping children safe while they are online. By educating children about the dangers of the internet, setting clear boundaries, and fostering healthy online communication, parents and caregivers can help keep children safe while they navigate the online world. It's important to have open and honest conversations with children about their online interactions, and to be available to offer guidance and support when needed. By keeping these key points in mind, parents and caregivers can ensure that children have positive and safe experiences while using the internet.

Chapter 12. Tips for parents on supporting kids' online privacy and safety.

As a parent, it's important to take an active role in supporting your children's online privacy and safety. The digital landscape is constantly evolving, and it can be difficult to stay informed about the latest technologies, apps, and trends. However, by educating yourself and setting boundaries and expectations, you can help your children navigate this landscape in a safe and responsible manner.

1. Set boundaries and expectations: Establish clear rules and guidelines for your children's online behavior. For example, you can set time limits for device use and monitor their activity. It's also important to discuss with them the type of content they can access and share online, and what is appropriate behavior online.

2. Educate yourself:

Stay informed about the latest technologies, apps, and online trends to better understand the digital landscape your children are navigating. There are many resources available online to help you stay informed and up-to-date on the latest online safety concerns.

3. Communicate openly:

Encourage your children to talk to you about their online experiences, both positive and negative. Listen actively and provide guidance and support when needed. It's important to foster open communication to ensure you are aware of any potential issues or concerns that arise.

4. Use parental controls:

Consider using built-in controls or third-party apps to help protect your children from inappropriate content and manage their device use. This can include features like content filters, time limits, and activity reporting.

5. Model good online behavior:

Children learn by example, so make sure you're setting a good one by practicing safe and responsible online behavior yourself. Avoid sharing personal information online, use privacy settings and use the same restrictions and guidelines you set for your kids with your own online accounts.

6. Teach online privacy:

Explain to your children the importance of maintaining online privacy and the dangers of sharing personal information. Teach them about the risks of talking to strangers online and when it is appropriate to share information. Also, make sure to educate them about using strong and unique passwords and security.

7. Emphasize empathy:

Encourage your children to be kind and respectful when interacting with others online. Remind them that words and actions online can have the same impact as they would in person. Teach them to think before they post, to be aware of their digital footprint, and to understand the consequences of their online behavior.

8. Encourage offline activities:

Help your children balance their time online with other activities, such as sports, hobbies, and spending time with friends and family in person. Encourage them to engage in a variety of activities that will help them grow and develop in different ways.

As a parent, you play a critical role in supporting your children's online privacy and safety. By setting boundaries and expectations, educating yourself, communicating openly, using parental controls, modeling good online behavior, teaching online privacy, emphasizing empathy and encouraging offline activities, you can help your children navigate the digital landscape in a safe and responsible manner. Remember that online safety is an ongoing process, so it's important to continuously monitor, educate and communicate with your children about the ever-evolving digital landscape.

Printed by Amazon Italia Logistica S.r.l.
Torrazza Piemonte (TO), Italy

44235865R00020

Printed in Great Britain
by Amazon

Thank you so very much for buying and reading my very first picture book. I hope you had fun meeting Fred.

Please can you leave a little review on Amazon or Goodreads, telling other people jus t how much fun you had meeting Fred, and learning all about kindness. It would really help me out, and it means I will be able to write more picture books for you to enjoy.

Thank you so much

Daniel Riding

There once was an octopus, his name was Fred.
He had purple skin, and he had lots of friends.
They were never mean, they were kind instead.
They were even nice, about Fred's hat, on his head.

So play they did, amongst the coral and reeds,
Kindness is really, all anyone needs,
So the lesson we learn, from our octopus friends.
Is that kindness is the best thing, for everyone in the end.

So before you say something, so terribly mean,
Be nice and be kind, don't be a mean bean.
Say something nice, and cheer up a friend,
It really is worth it all in the end.

"It's ok." he said, "I forgive you quite happily.

Now come on let's play, as one big family."

"We now know it's not nice, to be nasty or mean.
We want you as our friend, we hope you're still keen?"

Fred thought for a second, about running away
But that wouldn't help anyone, so he decided to stay.

They swam forward to join him, again they said sorry.
"We had a bad day, but that's not your worry.

We made you upset, for that we are sad,
We are sorry we called you names, for that we feel bad."

Fred gave a cheer, and did a spin,
He then heard a noise, come from behind him.
He turned around, and saw something bad.
It was the octopus kids, who had made him sad.

But before he could run, they saw him and screamed,
"Fred we are sorry, that we were so mean."
Fred was surprised, and Fred was shocked,
Their apology was nice, and it meant a lot,

He closed his eyes, He span around three times.
He kept going forward, then he opened his eyes.
And what did he find? A most wonderous space.
Fred was so happy, he had found his place.

It was the coral garden, at the oceans tip.
Where he was meant to go, on his school trip.
There was coral of purple, and coral of red,
There were even starfish, asleep in their beds.

"Turn left, turn right, and go straight on ahead.
You'll find some rocks, sat in the ocean bed.
Close your eyes, spin around three times.
Swim forward swim forward, then open your eyes."

"There you will find, a most wonderous space.
Here my friend, you will have found your place."
Fred was grateful, and he gave his thanks.
He hoped he was right, he would be happy, perhaps.

"Well hello young octopus, I believe you've been Sad.
I've been looking for you, I've found you, I'm glad.
You have done nothing but try your best.
Now it's time for you, to have a little rest."

"I'll tell you of a place, where your dreams come true.
Now listen carefully, here's what to do.
Keep swimming keep swimming, and try your best.
Look for the fish, who guard a chest."

He swam and he swam, through the plants and the reeds.
He swam though the rocks, and he swam through the weeds.

He said hello to the fish, as he swam on by.
He bumped into a turtle, who took him by surprise.

With that said, Fred turned to go.
He wasn't here to be bullied; he'll have you know.

So again, he swam, away from the crowd,
He didn't need all that nastiness around.

"Just please go home", they all shouted and spat.
"You look really daft in your stupid sad hat."
Well that was it, Fred had had enough.
"Don't be mean," he said, "don't pretend to be tough."

"I got a bit excited, when I saw you all,
I didn't mean to trip, I didn't mean to fall.
I only want to be friends, I wanted to be nice.
But you called me names, let me give you advice."

"Kindness is easy, kindness is free.
Have you any idea, what you did to me?
Name calling is mean, it makes you look bad,
It hurt my feelings, and made me sad."

"There is too much nastiness, in the world today,
I wanted to be friends, But I'll now go away
I made a mistake, and for that I am sorry,
But you don't need to be nasty, I'll leave, don't you worry."

And then he saw them, his classmates up ahead.
He slowed right now, and then he said.
"Hello, everybody, my name is Fred."
They looked at him and then they said.

"Oh no, it's you, the one who's a pain.
We don't want to hang out with you ever again.
You are very strange, and you are slightly odd.
We don't want you joining our squad."

When he arrived at School, he found he was late.
Everyone had left, and it didn't feel great.
He panicked a bit, he thought he'd lost his chance.
But he Shook himself and did a little dance.

"I can catch them up, as a matter of fact."
So, he Swam Super-fast, and nearly lost his hat.
He Swam through the ocean, as fast as he could.
His tentacles were tired, but he Still felt good.

So when school had finished, Fred went home.
He decided he wouldn't, spend the next day alone.
When day two arrived Fred made a wish.
So he swam through the bubbles, and sped past the fish.

"Today will be better", he shouted out loud.
"I'm going to be better; I'll be part of that crowd."
Today his classmates, were going on a trip.
To see the coral gardens, at the oceans tip.

Fred stepped back; he knew he'd done wrong.
But what they had said, had been a bit strong.
He knew he had upset them; he'd been a bit keen.
But did they really have to be so terribly mean?

Throughout the day, he was left on his own.
As his classmates swam away, he let out a groan.
For the rest of the day, Fred kept to himself.
Well this problem, wasn't going to fix itself.

"I am so very sorry; I didn't mean it." he said.
He stood up and shouted. "HELLO, my name is Fred!"
"We don't care who you are", his classmates said.
"Keep away from us, you silly bum head."

"What are you doing, you silly octopus?
Watch where you're going, you crashed into us."
Fred was gutted, and Fred was sad,
He'd made his classmates, so terribly mad.

He swam faster and faster, but before he could stop.
He crashed into the others and landed with a flop.

He shook his head; he felt a bit dizzy.
The other students were mad, and they seemed in a tizzy.

He swam as fast as he could, he wouldn't be late.
He sped through the ocean, like a horse out the gate.

He swam and he swam, and he then saw his school.
All the octopus kids, looked ever so cool,

When he awoke, he jumped out of bed.
He yelled out loud,

"MY NAME IS FRED"!

He said goodbye to his mum, and goodbye to his dad.
He was off to school, there was fun to be had.

Z

Z

Z

Z

Z

So, before it got too late, Fred closed his eyes.
And hoped he could sleep, before the sunrise.
And sleep he did, and he did dream.
That school was fun, and he was part of a team.

"I hope I'm not annoying, and I hope there's a crowd.
But sometimes I annoy people, because I can be quite loud.
I have lots of energy and can be a bit too much.
But I just want to play, and make friends, and such."

He tried not to get Sad, and he tried not to cry.
For tomorrow waS a new day, and he let out a Sigh.
He had hiS parentS, that waS nice for Sure.
But he wanted a pal, he wanted Something more.

But what he wanted most, was not to offend.
He wanted to meet, some special friends.
You see Fred was lonely, he was all alone.
He didn't have a friend, to call his own.

He wanted to learn, why he had eight legs.
What came first, chickens or eggs?
He wanted to know, lots and lots of things.
He wanted to learn about queens, and to learn about kings.

There once was an octopus, his name was Fred.
He had purple skin, and wore a hat on his head.
He couldn't sleep one night, as he snuggled up in bed.
He started school tomorrow, so he stayed awake instead.

Now this was silly, but Fred was excited.
His first day of school, and he was simply delighted.
What would he learn? How many friends would he make?
This was why he couldn't sleep, so he stayed wide awake.

Friendless Fred

Daniel Riding

For my niece, Alleah

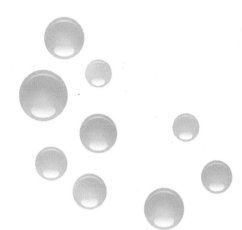